OUNCE

DICE

TRICE

OUNCE DiCE TRiCE

BY ALASTAIR REID

DRAWINGS BY BEN SHAHN

DEDICATION

For Michael, always and once again

Library of Congress Cataloging-in-Publication Data

Reid, Alastair, 1926–
    Ounce, dice, trice/by Alastair Reid with illustrations by Ben Shahn.
        p.   cm.
    Summary: A collection of old and new words, including those to be said
in singing moods, words for times of day, and rude names for nitwits.
Defines such words as gongoozler, tantony, and cosse.
    ISBN 0–8109–3655–0
    1. Wit and humor, Juvenile. 2. Vocabulary — Wit and humor.
[1. Wit and humor. 2. Vocabulary.] I. Shahn, Ben, 1898–1969, ill.
II. Title.
PN6163.R4   1991
428.1 — dc20   90–47601
                                                                    CIP

Published in 1991 by Harry N. Abrams, Incorporated, New York
A Times Mirror Company
All rights reserved. No part of the contents of this book may be
reproduced without the written permission of the publisher

Printed and bound in the United States of America

FOREWORD

Loosened from their clusters of meaning, words have a quite separate aura, a peculiar appearance and sound that is theirs alone. As children, we play with the sounds and shapes of words for pure fun long before we know what they mean. Later on, much of the pleasure we get from language — as poetry, as song, as fine prose — comes from the way it falls on our ear as well as our eye. Repeated over and over, any word can become mesmerizing to the mind, a kind of mantra. A sense of this is what distinguishes those who love language from those who only make use of it.

I put this book together some thirty years ago, out of a notebook I kept at the time and from the word games I played with a number of friends. The words are meant to be read aloud, by parents to children, or by adults to one another or to themselves. It is a quite arbitrary and random collection, meant only to give pleasure and, perhaps occasionally, to cause the shiver of surprise that can arise from certain words in place. I have resisted any temptation to tinker with the original text, for it is a starting point only, for the personal lists we make, for the words that families invent for themselves, for a way of using words as toys for the mind.

Alastair Reid

WORDS

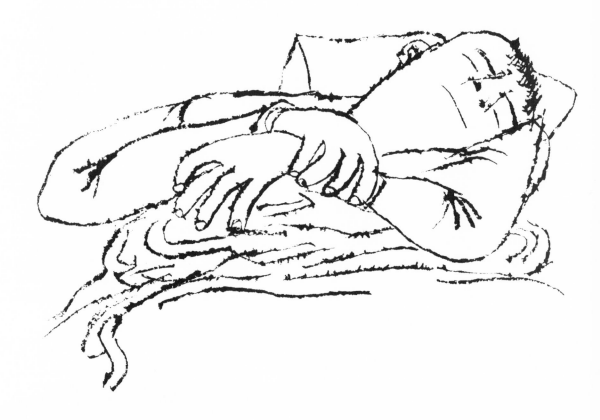

The way to get the feel of words is to begin with a sound and let it grow. **ZZZZ** is the sound of someone sleeping. From it, you easily move to **BUZZ** and **DIZZY,** and soon you have a list.

ZZZZ

BUZZ

DIZZY

FIZZLE

GUZZLE

BUZZARD

BAMBOOZLE

Or begin with **OG** and see what happens.

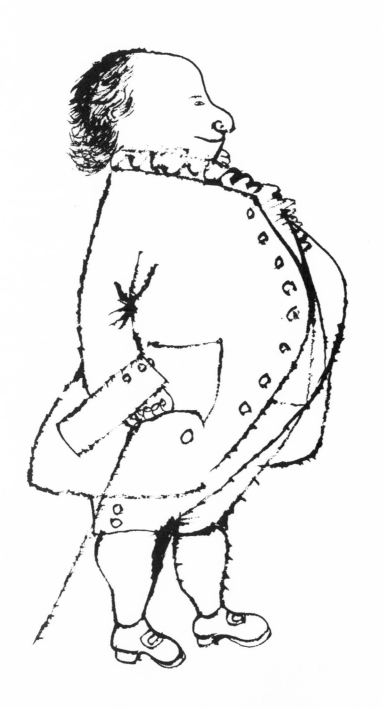

OG

FROG

OGLED

GOGGLE

GROGGY

TOBOGGAN

HEDGEHOG

And then you can make other lists by gathering together
words for noises or nightmares or things beginning with Q.
Here are some lists to guide you.

LIGHT WORDS

ARIEL

WILLOW

SPINNAKER

WHIRR

LISSOM

SIBILANT

PETTICOAT

NIMBLE

NIB

DUFFLE

BLUNDERBUSS

GALOSHES

BOWL

BEFUDDLED

MUGWUMP

PUMPKIN

CRUMB

BLOB

FLIT

FLUCTUATE

WOBBLE

WIGGLE

SHIVER

TIPTOE

PIROUETTE

TWIRL

TEETER

HOBNOB
BARLEY
DOG-EARED
HOPSCOTCH
WINDWARD

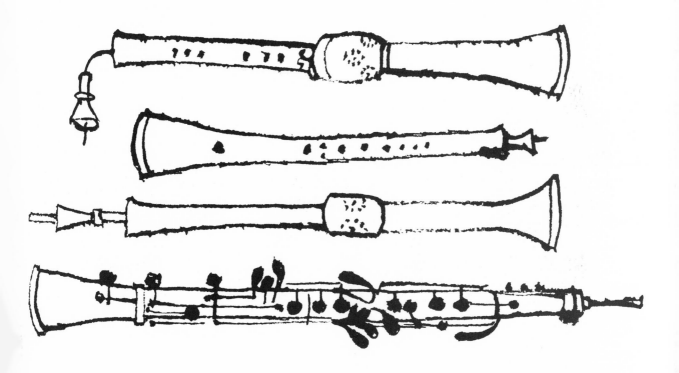

OAF
EGG
OBOE
NUTMEG
OBLONG

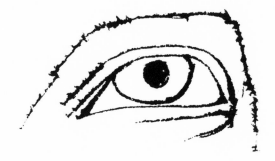
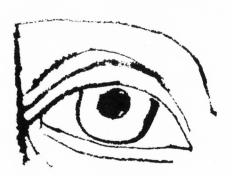

EYE
POOP
MINIM
LEVEL
KAYAK
MARRAM

DEIFIED   REFER

WORDS THAT READ BOTH WAYS

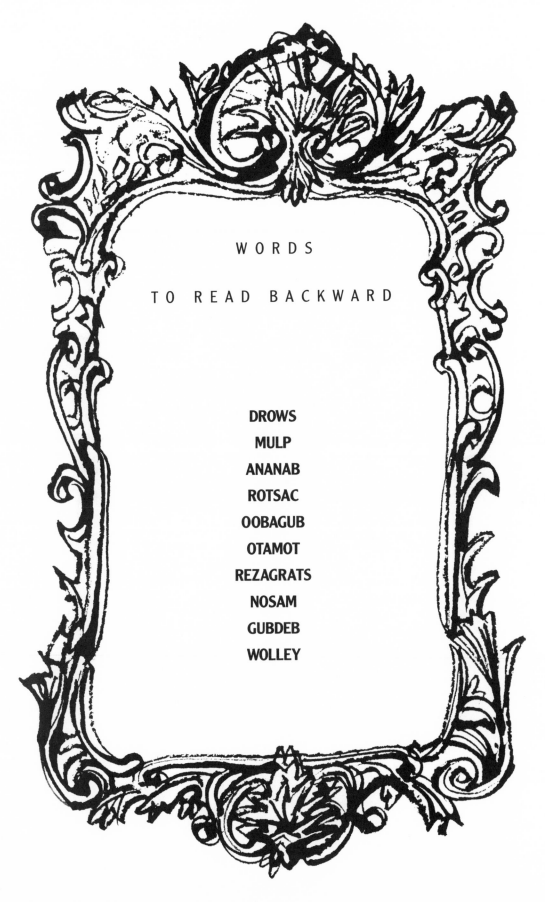

WORDS

TO READ BACKWARD

DROWS

MULP

ANANAB

ROTSAC

OOBAGUB

OTAMOT

REZAGRATS

NOSAM

GUBDEB

WOLLEY

SQUIFF

SQUIDGE

SQUAMOUS

SQUINNY

SQUELCH

SQUASH

SQUEEGEE

SQUIRT

SQUAB

BUG WORDS

HUMBUG

BUGBEAR

BUGABOO

BUGBANE

LADYBUG

BOGYBUG

BUGSEED

DAYPEEP

DAYSPRING

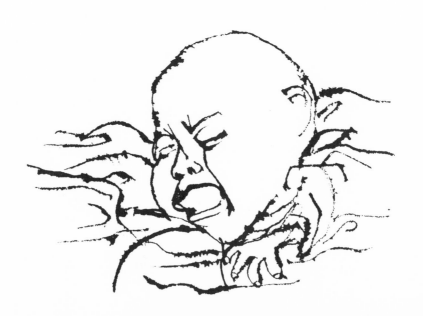

MERIDIAN

MAINDAY

DAYLIGONE

DIMITY

DUSK

OWLCRY

DEWFALL

GLOAMING

CLUSTERS

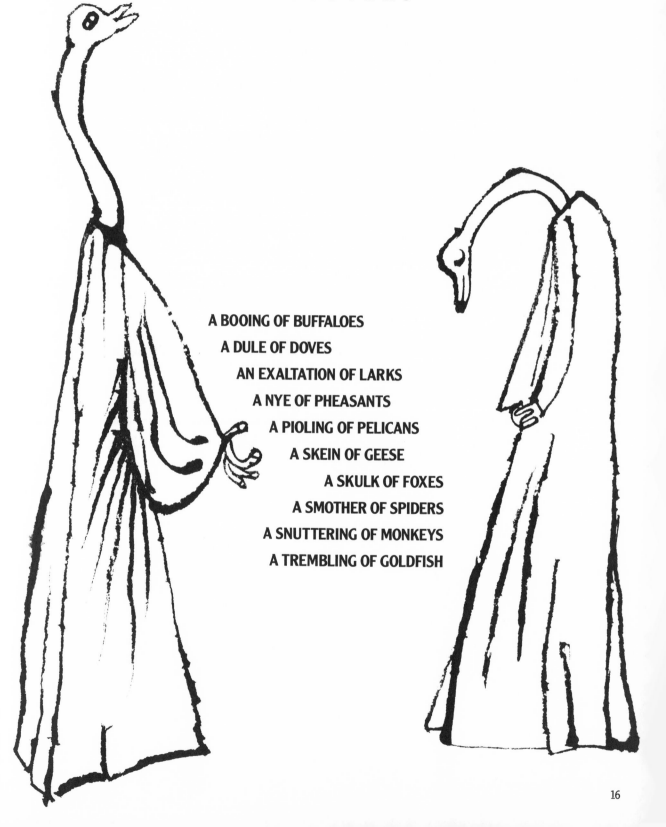

A BOOING OF BUFFALOES
A DULE OF DOVES
AN EXALTATION OF LARKS
A NYE OF PHEASANTS
A PIOLING OF PELICANS
A SKEIN OF GEESE
A SKULK OF FOXES
A SMOTHER OF SPIDERS
A SNUTTERING OF MONKEYS
A TREMBLING OF GOLDFISH

A BLUNDER OF BOYS

A GIGGLE OF GIRLS

A CONSTERNATION OF MOTHERS

A GRUMBLING OF BUSES

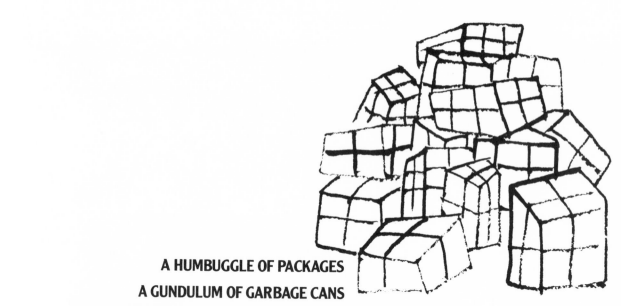

A HUMBUGGLE OF PACKAGES

A GUNDULUM OF GARBAGE CANS

A SCRIBBITCH OF PAPERS

A TUMBLETELL OF CHURCH BELLS

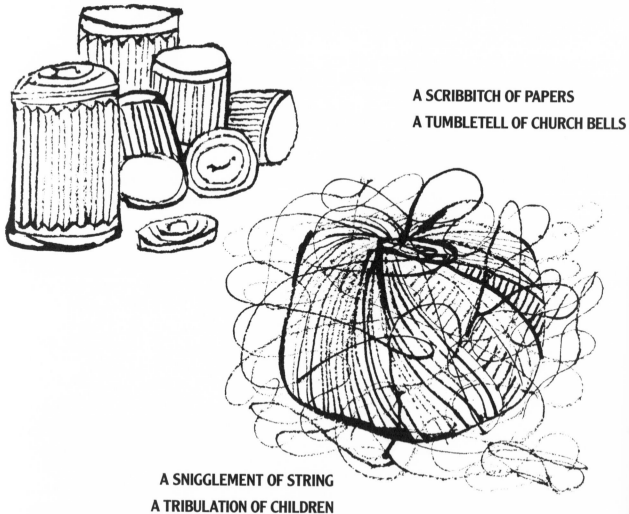

A SNIGGLEMENT OF STRING

A TRIBULATION OF CHILDREN

S O U N D S

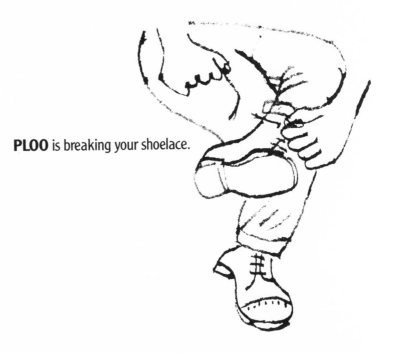

PLOO is breaking your shoelace.

MRRAAOWL
is what
cats
really say.

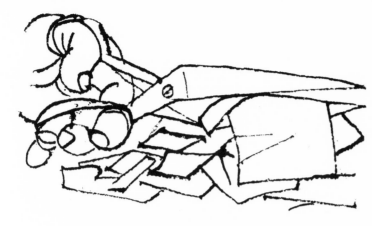

TRIS-TRAS

is scissors

cutting paper.

KINCLUNK is a car going over a manhole cover.

CROOMB is what

pigeons murmur

to themselves.

PHLOOPH is sitting suddenly

on a cushion.

NYO-NYO is speaking with your mouth full.

HARROWOLLOWORRAH is yawning.

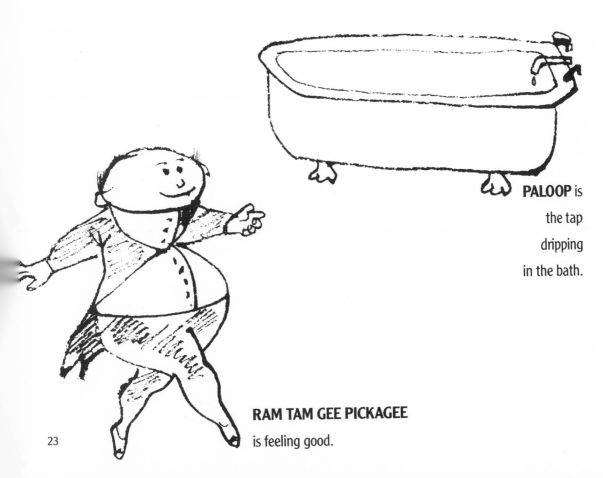

PALOOP is the tap dripping in the bath.

RAM TAM GEE PICKAGEE is feeling good.

NAMES

It is most important to be a good namer, since it falls to all of us at some time or other to name anything from a canary to a castle and since names generally have to last a long time. Here are some possible names.

NAMES FOR ELEPHANTS

WILBUR

BENDIGO

McGRAW

ORMOND

BRUCE

ROBERTSON

WENDELL TUBB

DUFF

DEUTERONOMY

NAMES FOR CATS

SYBIL

CHESTER

LISSADEL

GRICE

MILDRED

FELICITY

ASTRID

JAMES BUDGE

TWEE

SINBAD

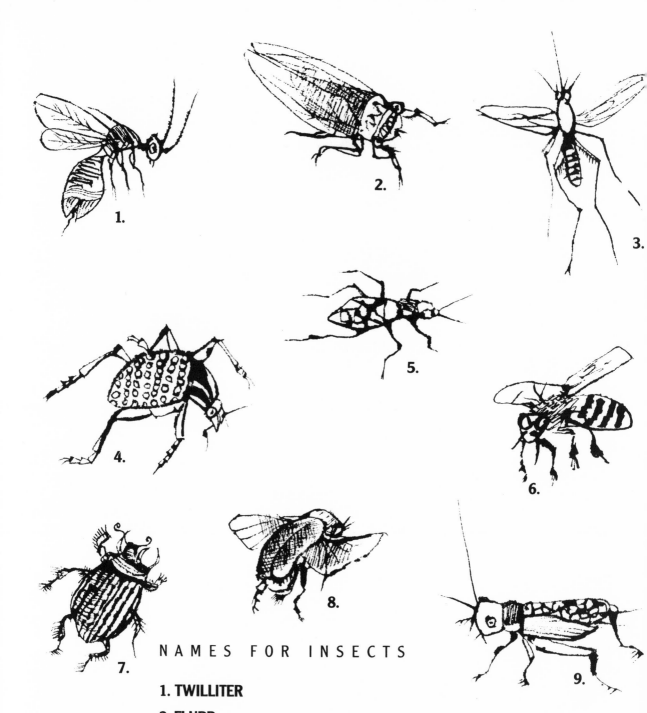

N A M E S   F O R   I N S E C T S

1. TWILLITER

2. FLURR

3. TRISTRAM   **4. LIMLET**

5. TILLTIN

6. SUMMERSBY   **7. THRIMM**

8. LEGLIDDY

9. UGWOB

NAMES FOR WHALES

HUGH   **BLODGE**   **BARNABY**   **HAMISH**

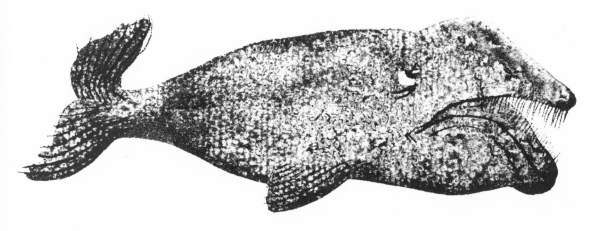

CHUMLEY   **MURDO**   **CHAM**   **OKUM**   **SUMP**

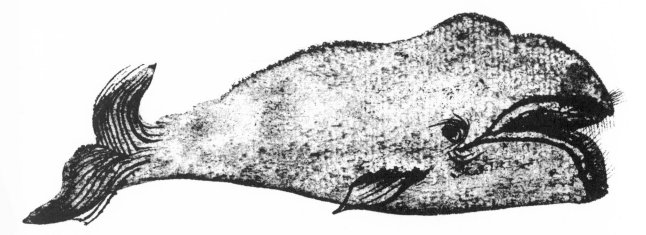

HUGG HOUSE	**THE BOBBINS**
BROADMEADOWS	**DEERSDEN**
WINDYGATES	**SMITHEREENS**
HOPESHAWS	**OLD HULLABALOO**
SMUDGIN'S NOB	**DRUMJARGON**
LONG STILT LANE	**THE SHIVERS**

PEE DEE
PARSNIP
TWEED
TOMBIGBEE
OUSE
SHOSHONE
CHINDWIN
CAM
OKEFINOKEE
APP
AAR
URR

RUDE NAMES

RAPSCALLION
FLIBBERTIGIBBET
FUSSBUDGET
COYSTRIL
TAYSTRIL
JOSKIN
BUMPKIN
CLOAF
CLODHOPPER
SLAMMERKIN

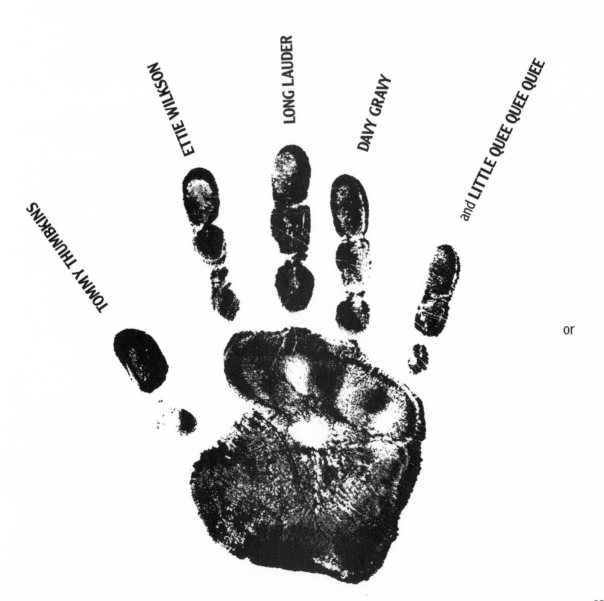

ETTIE WILKSON

LONG LAUDER

DAVY GRAVY

and LITTLE QUEE QUEE QUEE QUEE

TOMMY THUMBKINS

or

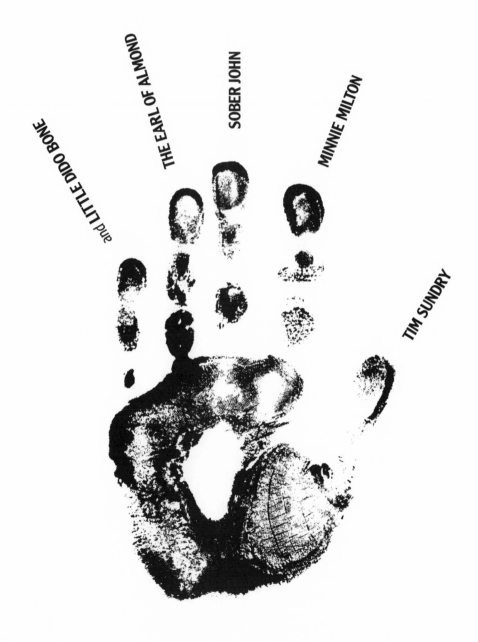

and LITTLE DIDO BONE

THE EARL OF ALMOND

SOBER JOHN

MINNIE MILTON

TIM SUNDRY

Ani's Hand

NAMES FOR TWINS

Each pair of twins,

rabbits or dogs,

children or frogs,

has to have names

that are almost the same

(to show that they're twins)

but are different too;

so here's what you do.

Find double words, like

HIGGLEDY-PIGGLEDY

(good names for pigs)

or **SHILLY AND SHALLY**
or **DILLY AND DALLY**
or **KNICK AND KNACK.**

NAMBY AND PAMBY

are better for poodles;

WHING-DING for swallows;
MISTY AND MOISTY
and **WISHY AND WASHY**

especially for fish.

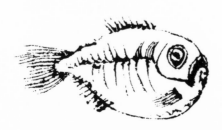

Call twin kittens

INKY AND PINKY

or **HELTER AND SKELTER,**

or **PELL AND MELL.**

(It's easy to tell

they are twins if their names

have a humdrum sound.)

CRINKUM AND CRANKUM

are perfect for squirrels, like

HANKY AND PANKY

or **FIDDLE AND FADDLE;**

but **MUMBO AND JUMBO**

are mainly for elephants.

(AIRY AND FAIRY

would never suit **THEM.)**

WILLY AND NILLY

will fit almost any twins.

HUBBLE AND BUBBLE

or **HODGE AND PODGE**

or **ROLY AND POLY**

are mainly for fat twins.

CHITTER AND CHATTER
or **JINGLE AND JANGLE**
or **PITTER AND PATTER,**
of course, are for noisy twins.

Further than that, there's
HARUM AND SCARUM,
or **HOCUS AND POCUS,**
or **HEEBIE AND JEEBIE,**
but these are peculiar,
and have to be used, like
MIXTY AND MAXTY,
for very **ODD** pairs....
You see what begins
when you have to name twins.

COUNTERS

Instead of counting **ONE, TWO, THREE,** make up your own numbers, as shepherds used to do when they had to count sheep day in, day out. You can try using these sets of words instead of numbers when you count to ten.

OUNCE

DICE

TRICE

QUARTZ

QUINCE

SAGO

SERPENT

OXYGEN

NITROGEN

DENIM

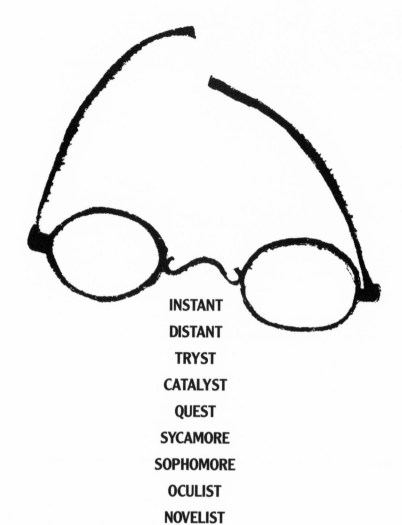

INSTANT
DISTANT
TRYST
CATALYST
QUEST
SYCAMORE
SOPHOMORE
OCULIST
NOVELIST
DENTIST

ARCHERY
BUTCHERY
TREACHERY
TAPROOM
TOMB
SERMON
CINNAMON
APRON
NUNNERY
DENSITY

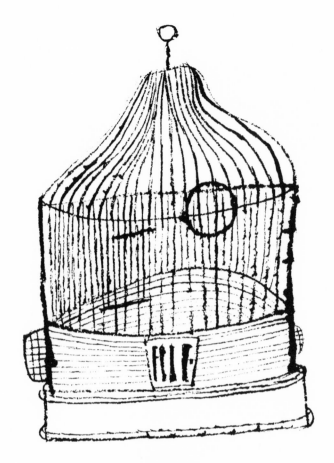

ACREAGE

BROKERAGE

CRIBBAGE

CARTHAGE

CAGE

SINK

SENTIMENT

OINTMENT

NUTMEG

DOOM

GARLANDS

Here are some odd words, either forgotten or undiscovered, each leading to the next and bringing you back eventually to the beginning.

What is a **TINGLE-AIREY?**

A **TINGLE-AIREY** is a hand organ, usually played on the street by the turning of a handle, and often decorated with mother-of-pearl or **PIDDOCK** shells.

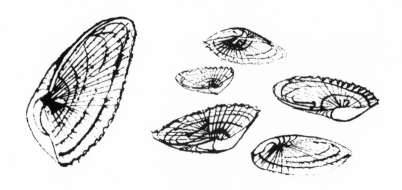

What are **PIDDOCKS**?

PIDDOCKS are little mollusks

that bore holes in rocks and wood,

or in the **BREASTSUMMERS** of buildings.

What is a **BREASTSUMMER**?

A **BREASTSUMMER** is a great beam supporting

the weight of a wall, and never found in a **GAZEBO**.

What is a **GAZEBO?**

A **GAZEBO** is a freestanding structure
looking out on a view, often of
ornamental gardens and **COTONEASTERS.**

What is a **COTONEASTER?**

A **COTONEASTER** is a kind of
flowering shrub,
a favorite of **MUMRUFFINS.**

What is a **MUMRUFFIN?**

A **MUMRUFFIN** is a long-tailed tit that often visits
bird feeders in winter for its share of **POBBIES.**

What are **POBBIES?**

POBBIES are small pieces of bread **THRUMBLED** up with
milk and fed to birds and baby animals.

What is **THRUMBLED?**

THRUMBLED is squashed together.
Ants thrumble round a piece of bread,
and crowds in streets thrumble round **GONGOZZLERS.**

What is a **GONGOZZLER?**

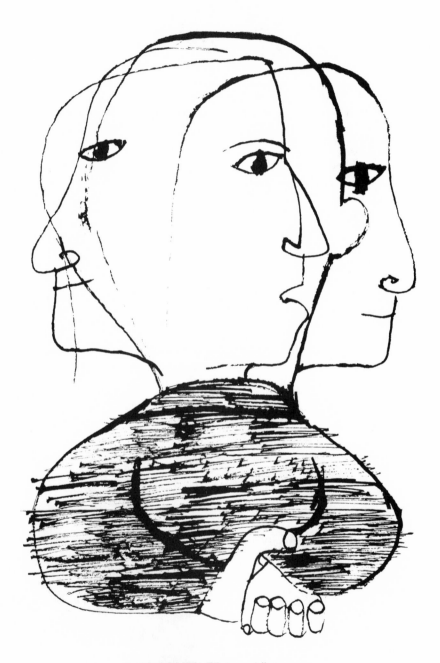

A **GONGOZZLER** is an idle person
who is always stopping in the street
and staring at a curious object
like a **TINGLE-AIREY.**

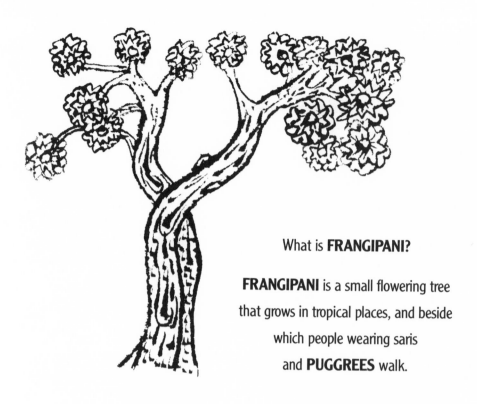

What is **FRANGIPANI?**

FRANGIPANI is a small flowering tree
that grows in tropical places, and beside
which people wearing saris
and **PUGGREES** walk.

What is a **PUGGREE?**

A **PUGGREE** is a light scarf
worn over a hat to protect
the **PAX WAX** from the sun.

What is the **PAXWAX?**

The **PAXWAX** is the tendon at the back
of the neck that supports the head,
and which flushes red when people
are in a **TIRRIVEE.**

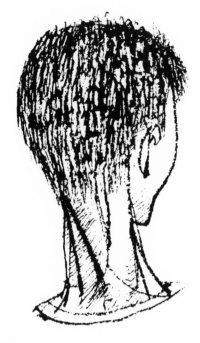

What is a **TIRRIVEE?**

A **TIRRIVEE** is a temper.
Mothers go into a **TIRRIVEE** over
the **JIGGERY-POKERY** of children.

What is **JIGGERY-POKERY?**

JIGGERY-POKERY is trickery
or mischief or hanky-panky
on the part of children,
such as pretending to be deaf or
teasing a **TANTONY.**

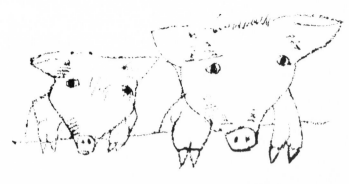

What is a **TANTONY?**

A **TANTONY** is the smallest pig
in a litter, so called after Saint Anthony, the patron saint
of swineherds. Small creatures are usually given
special names, like kittens or cygnets or **QUICKLINGS.**

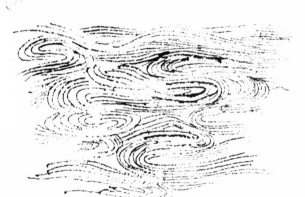

What are **QUICKLINGS?**

QUICKLINGS are young insects
which in summer dance
in the air in clouds and
catch the light, looking like **MOONGLADE.**

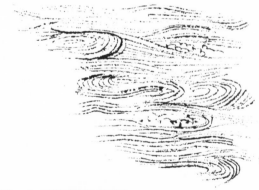

What is **MOONGLADE?**

MOONGLADE is the track of dancing broken light
left on the sea at **DIMITY** by the moon.

What is **DIMITY?**

DIMITY, besides being a fine cotton fabric,
is the time of day when the daylight dims,
the time when, in hot countries, men and women
walk in the coolth beside the **FRANGIPANI.**

What is a **HAMBURGLER?**

A **HAMBURGLER** is a hamburger
that you creep downstairs
and eat in the middle of the
night when you wake up hungry.
MIM people never eat **HAMBURGLERS.**

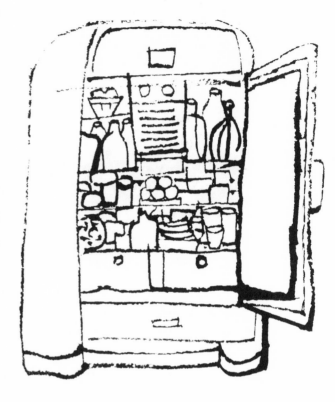

What are **MIM** people?

MIM people are very proper people
who always sit with
their fingertips together and
their lips pursed tight,
who always do the right thing,
and who disapprove.
MIM people have **WORGS**
in their gardens.

What is **WORG?**

A **WORG** is a plant that never grows.
There is practically always one
WORG in a row of plants.
You can tell it by the
GNURR on its leaves.

What is **GNURR?**

GNURR is the substance that
collects after periods of time
in the bottom of pockets
or in the cuffs of trousers.
GNURR is a smaller variety
of **OOSSE.**

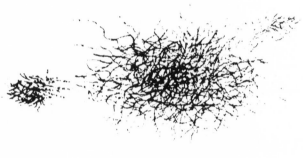

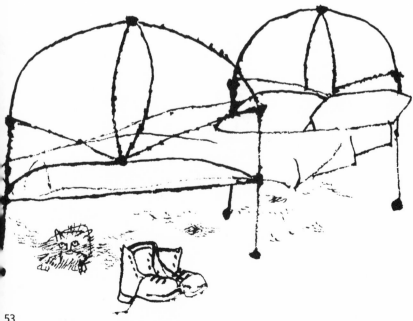

What is **OOSSE?**

OOSSE is the airy,
furry stuff that
ultimately gathers
under beds and
GONOMONIES.
It is also called
TRILBIES, KITTENS,
or **DUST-BUNNIES.**

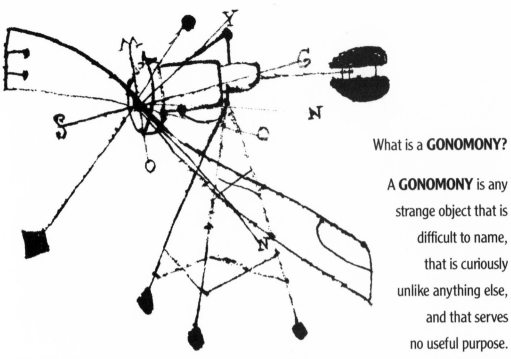

What is a **GONOMONY?**

A **GONOMONY** is any
strange object that is
difficult to name,
that is curiously
unlike anything else,
and that serves
no useful purpose.
GONOMONIES abound in the houses of **GLOTS.**

What is a **GLOT?**

A **GLOT** is a person who cannot bear to waste anything,
who stuffs his attic full of treasures that nobody else wants,
and who always eats
the last chocolate
in the box.
GLOTS can be
recognized by
the **POOSE** on
their noses.

What is a **POOSE?**

A **POOSE** is a drop that stays on
the end of the nose and glistens.
It happens to ordinary people
when they have colds,
or when they come out of the sea
for a **CHITTERING-BITE.**

What is a **CHITTERING-BITE?**

A **CHITTERING-BITE** is a snack eaten after a cold swim
to keep the teeth from chattering. It may consist of
anything from an apple to a piece of leftover **HAMBURGLER.**

If you want to call for silence, say

MUMBUDGET

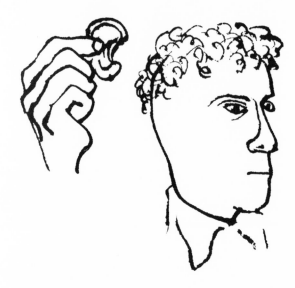

If you want to
change the subject, say
PONSONBY

If you want to stop a game that you are playing, say
BARLEY
PAX
KING'S X
KING'S RANSOM
FINS
KEYS
UNCLE
or **CRIK-CRAK**

And if someone tells you
something you don't believe,
look at him steadily and say
FIRKYDOODLE
FUDGE
or **QUOZ**

WORDS WORTH SAVING

NAMES

FAMILY WORDS

PRIVATE WORDS